MIRROR *Work*

FROM PAIN TO PURPOSE:

A 21 DAY

JOURNEY TO WHOLENESS

WRITTEN BY:

CHRISTINA KING-ROGERS

Published by
Live Limitless Authors Academy & Publishing Co.
Publishing@sierrarainge.com
www.livelimitless.co

Christina King-Rogers
Contact Information:
Website: www.wholeinternationalinc.org
Bookings@wholeinternationalinc.org

Email:
Printed in the United States of America
Cover Design by: Adam I. Wade

ISBN: 978-1-952903-14-4

TABLE OF CONTENTS

Christina King-Rogers

DEDICATION

To My Father Michael Jerome King and Brother Charles King Boyd… as long as I live I will make sure you are never forgotten; I will continue to make you both proud.

ACKNOWLEDGEMENTS

First giving honor to God and My Lord and Savior Jesus Christ who is truly the head of my life, the lover of my soul and the reason for my being.

I would like to give honor to my amazing husband Mercedes Rogers and children (Jayda, Christian, Aaliyah, and Neriah for your unfailing love, patience and understanding that I have not only been called to be your wife/mom but to also serve God's people. This spiritual walk comes with many sacrifices but I couldn't have asked for a better family to share in this journey. I love you all so much.

I would like to thank my Mother Claudette Short for living a life of Holiness and Righteousness and setting a standard through your prayer walk, you have stayed on your knees for your family. You have been such a huge support system and listening ear during this process of writing. Our daily talks and prayers is what has gotten me through some of my toughest days. I thank God for you every day.

I love you mommy.

To my prayer partner, spiritual mentor and dearest friend Pastor Christie McKinney Evans without your spiritual guidance I wouldn't have had the courage to take the leap and write the book!!!! 3 years ago you prophetically spoke to me while having lunch together concerning writing and here is the manifestation. I am eternally grateful to God for our friendship.

To the "Be Made Whole Ministry Family" it is because of our virtual weekly broadcast that has deeply inspired me to write this book in order to be the compelling voice that pushes you beyond your limitations.

I also dedicate this book to all women from all different walks of life who have lost their sense of purpose and have struggled to regain their identity and confidence. I wrote this book to help you affirm and reclaim who you are in Christ.

AN "OPEN LETTER" TO THE WOMAN BRAVE ENOUGH TO TAKE A LOOK IN THE MIRROR.

"I SEE YOU" and I know when you read that you were probably thinking, "'girl bye, how can you see me when you have never met me?" You're probably thinking that I'm being pretentious and I'm sure you're thinking to yourself that I don't know what you're going through, what you've been through or the scars that you bare and perhaps you're right. I mean, I don't know you from a can of paint, I don't know the depths of pain and hurt that you have had to endure., I am unaware of the many tears that you have cried night after night, all the times that you broke your back bending over backwards to serve those around you, giving all of yourself, emotionally, physically, spiritually and even financially to others who said they loved you and were supposed to shield and protect you but in return, instead all that you received was a slap in the face; the lack of reciprocity tends to leave residue of resentment and rejection.

As you begin to read through the pages and you find yourself feeling vulnerable wondering how can I possibly know about your feelings of uncertainty and the many doubts about yourself that you battle daily, you may have never opened up to anyone before about your trust issues, or the emotional heaviness that accompanies the internal battle of warring with feelings of unworthiness. There are many painful scenarios that we bottle up because the memory of the trauma is often too much to bare. Who have you told that you were violated as a child and robbed of your innocence? Or have you opted to be misunderstood, knowing that due to the trauma of your past, you would look for love in all the wrong places, seeking and searching for someone to love you genuinely and to fill that empty void deep down in your soul. It's a lot easier to repeat the cycle of broken and toxic relationships, than to take the lid off of the pain you kept bottled up for years. The truth is, you desire the close intimacy of a healthy and loving relationship, but you've never seen healthy romance modeled in your life and all those that you dared to love have left you broken and bruised.

Well, honestly nobody had to tell me your deepest darkest secrets. No 'one had to illustrate your personal despair or spell out the intricacies of your emotional injury, because if we're speaking honestly, the pain points and challenges that I articulate in this book were crafted from my personal perspective. You see, as women we may be in different boats, but we often find ourselves in the same storm, I was that girl that hid behind her trust issues, masked rejection, covered my low self-worth, and recycled broken relationships and childhood trauma.

It wasn't until I truly stepped into my identity in Christ that I was able to experience a total life transformation. It was then and only then that I recognized the power of being a victor rather than a victim.

If I am totally honest with you, my change didn't happen overnight, and neither did it happen because others wanted me to change.

It happened for me through deep meditation in the word of God, prayer, counseling and self-evaluation.

I know what it's like to suffer in silence, repeat toxic cycles and carry the heaviness of living beneath your potential. I know what it's like to struggle but still wrestle with the belief that there is so much more to life than settling. I made a decision to rise up because I refused to stay stuck and you can too. It all begins with a choice. You must decide today that you will no longer accept less than God's best in your life; that you deserve healing and wholeness and you are willing to do the work required to release yesterday's pain so that you can embrace the peace, love, joy and possibilities that today has to offer.

So, if you are ready; for the next 21 days, I am going to challenge you to disrupt the limiting beliefs that keep you playing small. I am going to push you to become the most authentic version of yourself. This book is going to give you the tools, the insight and ignite spiritual strength through scripture to help you stand in your power so that you can uncover your true identity and live a life full of freedom and fulfillment. The woman you see today in the mirror will never be the same.

This is your moment and this is your time! My prayer for you during this journey is that you will be willing to let go of the pain of your past so that you can stretch forward to grab the new life that is ahead of you.

I love you so very much and I am rooting for you. This is your season to uncover, heal, understand, celebrate and love yourself like never before. This is the time to assess your worth and commit to the Mirror Work.

INTRODUCTION

Remember Who You Are!

As you go through this book and turn the page we will be doing a lot of mirror work. It's important for me to bring you back to your remembrance, so I want you to step into the mirror and if you can't see it for yourself, I'm going to allow you to use my lens, furthermore not even my lens but the lens of God. Who were you before the children, before the betrayal, before the divorce, before the grief, before the disappointment? Who were you before the scars, are you able to see yourself before the heartache?

CHAPTER 1
ENOUGH

SELF- WORTH, SELF-PRESERVATION & SELF- CARE

How has the lack of self-worth shown up in your life?

Have you ever said to yourself or even thought, "Am I enough?" Have you ever wondered if others would accept you? Do you get down on yourself when you make mistakes? Do you normally feel small or insignificant when around certain people?

Low self-worth usually manifests as self-sabotage and it paralyses your potential.

When you fail to see yourself in the highest regard it can stop you from achieving greatness. How you view yourself through your intrinsic lens is often a reflection of the quality of your thoughts, your belief system and your personal value assessment. A poor personal perspective t can be brought on by negative self-talk or being too overly critical of yourself; also allowing others opinions and voice to have way too much leverage in your life and what tends to happen when you take on low self-worth; if you are not careful, Sadness, depression and even anxiety can creep in subtly.

Someone in the Bible that could relate to feelings of low self-worth was "The Woman with the Alabaster Box" she isn't actually named in the Bible but she made a huge impact and impression on Jesus.

In reading and reflecting on this story, "Hope" is clearly the driving force for the woman with the alabaster box.

In the book of *Luke 7:37-50* it talks about how this woman was a sinner and everyone in the town knew it including Jesus. However, what I most admire about this story is that Jesus used a parable when speaking to his disciple about her; many of her spectators and accusers couldn't see past her mistakes and actually wanted Jesus to hold it against her; but God had a plan. The woman had already known that her reputation was public news and so did Jesus. Guilt, shame and hurt had plagued her, but she heard that Jesus would be stopping by a nearby location to eat. She figured that this would be her opportunity to receive restoration. No words were used when she was in the presence of the Lord. She kissed his feet, cried, anointed his feet with precious oil and used her hair as a towel. In that moment, nothing else mattered, that was her moment and those feelings of not being enough or even worthy of God's love were now gone because she was in the presence of the one that made her *WORTHY*.

Past mistakes and failed relationships do not define who you are. Our merit lies more in who we are becoming rather than who we've been. There is redemptive power that dwells in developing our future self. God is calling you to your higher self. If you are reading this book; you may have done something in your past that you are not proud of. There may be circumstances in your life that keep you from seeing your worth, but remember failure is not your final destination, it's a moment in your life that has allowed you to gain transformative experience. You deserve to experience the bliss that accompanies change. You are worthy of living a life that reflects healing and wholeness. You are enough.

Your self-worth allows you to position yourself not only to profit but to prosper. When you're clear about who you are, you will put everybody else on notice, especially the people around you. Too often we wait for the people around us to validate us, or you may have said to yourself "I'll feel worthy if I get a husband" or I'll feel worthy if they like me or accept me. Choose yourself and then establish what you will and will not tolerate. True growth requires that you understand what your strengths are, what your passion is, what your purpose is and then place more value on those things and how you can positively impact others.

How many people are you going to be around that you can touch in a fruitful way? That's the real flex sis, there is no real value in what you wear or the things you acquired, and materialism is a fleeting sense of vanity.

Why haven't you started the business venture that you've been dreaming of? Is it comparison or lack of confidence that continues to haunt you? When will you take life by the hands? As long as you are moving and shaking in your life, you will always have critics and naysayers who will try to tell you what you can't do, or who you can't become. Always remember that, "you are enough!"

The day-to-day decisions that you make are attributed to your core values and the beliefs that you hold about yourself.

MIRROR MOMENT:

Do you see yourself in the woman in the alabaster box story?

_____

_____

_____

How does knowing or hearing this story make you feel?

_____

_____

_____

How has your view on yourself impacted your decisions?

_____

_____

_____

Do you allow men or women to mishandle you or even mistreat you?

_____

_____

_____

Do you not stand up for yourself?

_____

_____

_____

Do you speak up for yourself?

_____

_____

_____

Do you demand your worth in relationships or business transactions?

_____

_____

_____

Do you tie your worth to how much you can do for others?

_____

_____

_____

What about how much money you can make?

_____

_____

_____

When you're not working do you feel less than if you are not getting applause?

_____

_____

_____

VALUE ASSESSMENT:

Here is a quick checklist to see if you are honoring your worth?

- Do you put the needs of others before yourself?

- Are you a people pleaser?

- Do you have little to no boundaries?

- Are you always saying YES to things that you don't have the capacity or bandwidth to say yes too?

- How strong is your NO?

CHAPTER 2
I'M WORTH IT

MIRROR OF SELF PRESERVATION

"Overextending yourself and overcompensating in your relationships it doesn't make you any more loving or any more kind it just reveals that you have an issue with truly loving and honoring yourself enough to say NO"

~Anonymous

Self-preservation is really about making hard decisions in the face of pressure. It's about making decisions that put yourself at the forefront, and to protect the purpose and calling of God in your life.

One person in the bible that can relate all too well with self-preservation is Esther. Esther's parents died when she was a child and she became an orphan who was adopted and raised by her uncle Mordecai.

One day the King Xerxes threw a very lavish party. On the final day of the festivities, he called for his queen, Vashti. The king was eager to flaunt his wife's beauty to his guests. However, Vashti refused to appear before Xerxes. Filled with rage, he removed Queen Vashti from the throne.

He then sought out a new queen by hosting a royal beauty pageant. It was then that Esther was chosen for the throne. Her uncle Mordecai became a well-known official.

Soon Mordecai uncovered a plot to assassinate the king. He told Esther about the conspiracy, and she reported it to King Xerxes, and gave credit to Mordecai. The plot was thwarted and Mordecai's act of kindness was preserved in the chronicles of the king.

During that time, the king's highest official was a very evil man named Haman. He hated the Jews, especially Mordecai, because Mordecai had refused to bow down to him.

Haman devised a plan to have every Jew in Persia killed. The king agreed to his plan to kill the Jewish people on a specific day. Meanwhile, Mordecai learned of the plot and shared it with Esther, challenging her to not only think of herself but to think about the future of her people.

> *"Do not think that because you are in the king's house you alone of all the Jews will escape. For if you remain silent at this time, relief and deliverance for the Jews will arise from another place, but you and your father's family will perish. And who knows but that you have come to your royal position for such a time as this?" (Esther 4:13-14, NIV)*

Queen Esther urgently called for fasting and praying amongst her people because they needed the assistance of God .In this moment she could have only thought of herself and not consider the fate of her people, but here she understood God had preserved her and promoted her to queen in order to save her people. Risking her own life, brave Esther approached the king with a request.

Mordecai was promoted to Haman's high position and Jews were granted protection throughout the land. The people celebrated God's tremendous deliverance, and the joyous festival of Purim was instituted.

Self-Preservation is all about making sure you are clear about who you are, what you have been called to do, and most importantly setting firm boundaries, so when others have to lean on you, you are not producing from an empty cup, and you are not overexerting yourself to fit the expectations of others. In that moment of Esther's life she knew that in order to preserve herself she had to think of her family and her people; but so often we forget to take care of ourselves at the expense of pleasing others.

It is all about knowing when to say "Yes" and when to say "NO" and God will always be there to lead you through the spirit of discernment.

This is applicable in relationships as well. Sometimes people stay in relationships that drain them, fail to serve them, or with those who are incapable of honoring their boundaries. Oftentimes it's because the relationship provides some sort of security, or you feel as though the other part needs you so you suppress your true feelings knowing that the relationship really has no true value and it leaves you feeling empty, depleted and drained.

Self-preservation is the ability to detach from things that no longer serve you. It's also a way to honor yourself by recognizing that when you are serving others from a full cup you will offer them the best part of you.

MIRROR MOMENT:

How often do you stay in places, connections or relationships that no longer serve you?.

_____

_____

_____

_____

_____

_____

_____

_____

_____

_____

_____

_____

VALUE ASSESSMENT:

Here are some self-preservation tips in order to show up for yourself:

- Tune into your feelings
- Be direct and intentional
- Give yourself permission to rest when you need to and say no when you want to
- Practice self-awareness
- Make self-care a priority
- Seek support and be willing to receive it

CHAPTER 3
SELF CARE FOR MY SOUL

MIRROR OF SELF CARE

What Fills You Up?

Self-care is the most important way to boost and maintain both your emotional and physical wellbeing. But we tend to neglect it due to a lack of time, and this

Negatively impacts the lives of those who do not make sure they are putting themselves first.

Think of some ways where you can show up for yourself. In the modern world that we live in there are various messages through the media telling us to put ourselves first? What do you do in order to relax and refresh?

_____

_____

_____

_____

_____

_____

What does self-care look like to you?

_____

_____

_____

_____

_____

_____

_____

Is it long hot baths, stealing away to read a good book, is it a deluxe Mani/Pedi, a walk in the park alone, binge watching your favorite Netflix movie or series?

_____

_____

_____

_____

Is it spiritual meditation in prayer and studying God's word, is it a massage, is it leaving white space on your calendar in order to create memorable moments and finally put that to do list away?

Self-care is not selfish but self-preservation. In the word of God it says *"Don't you know that you yourselves are God's temple and that God's Spirit dwells in your midst? If anyone destroys God's temple, God will destroy that person; for God's temple is sacred, and you together are that temple." 1 Corinthians 3:16-17 (NIV).*

We have to be diligent in taking care of our bodies and minds for the sake of God because it belongs to him and so we can live a healthy, peaceful and fulfilled life.

First you have to get clear about what fills you up and what drains you!

Many of you reading this book are just like me. I am a woman that wears many hats; I am a wife, mother, evangelist, host, business owner, servant, daughter, sister, and friend. The list goes on and on but I learned the hard way that none of this matters if I'm not accountable to myself.

In 2009 when I started to experience extreme anxiety, fatigue, shortness of breath and a mass growth in my neck (an enlarged goiter) that was a sure sign and indication that I had neglected to take care of myself. I knew these symptoms existed but I was too afraid to seek medical attention and too overly concerned with other things which in turn resulted in Stage 3 thyroid cancer. I thought my life was over so I went into a state of shock and depression. I beat myself up about what I could or should have done. All of this would have been alleviated had I taken more time for self-care and analysis. I failed to take my health seriously and as a result I paid for it through radiation treatments, several surgeries and 2 full years in and out of the hospital to keep the cancer from coming back.

Over the course of time, what being sick and facing death has taught me is that I can't take care of others unless I am taking care of myself first mentally, physically and emotionally.

Here are 10 ways to daily exercise self-care and take better care of yourself.

- Self-care means knowing who you are and knowing your limits.

- Self-care means getting the sleep you need and knowing how and when to rest.

- Self-care means making sure that you are well mentally, emotionally and physically.

- Self-care means saying NO when you would otherwise say YES.

- Self-care means giving some thought to changing a difficult work situation.

- Self-care means taking time to get regular doctor checkups.

- Self-care means identifying what you enjoy doing and what's fun for you and making a serious effort to integrate it into your day.

- Self-care means feeding on the word of God and mediation in prayer and supplication to strengthen the inner you.

- Self-care means making time for exercising.

- Self-care means setting healthy boundaries and limitations.

CHAPTER 4
IT HAPPENED FOR ME!

MIRROR OF REJECTION

How has your rejection shown up in your life? Who told
you that you weren't worthy?

> Me: It is my fault! I am to blame! I am the reason
> that things never work out!

> Them: You are the reason things always fail! I wish
> I never met you. I hate you. I don't like you.

Do these phrases sound familiar? Sometimes we can
rehearse certain things to ourselves and it becomes a part
of how we show up in the world.

This is how rejection can play out in your life.

Rejection of self and by others can leave you feeling
low, dismissed, overlooked, abandoned and even
forsaken, someone that could relate to rejection in the

Bible first hand is Hagar; she was a Egyptian girl and handmaiden of Sarah the wife of Abraham (*Genesis 161:13*) once Sarah saw that she could not bear children she gave Hagar to her husband so that she conceived seed through her; but that plan backfired and instead of Sarah being happy that her plan succeeded; she was filled with discontentment, jealousy and rage toward Hagar and sent her away used and rejected. But, what I most love about this story is that God didn't leave her there in that place of brokenness, he actually sent an Angel to let her know that she indeed was pregnant but he also restored her confidence in knowing that she wasn't alone and that "He Saw Her" where she was now and even gave her a promise and hope for the future, not only for her but also her unborn child.

There will be times where the rejection of man is a sure sign of the redirection of God. I can think back over a few times in my life that I would work hard towards my business endeavors where I would pour my entire self into a project all for the wrong reason "validation and approval" trying to prove to myself and even others that I had worth and value. I would dedicate hours upon hours of my time and resources investing all of my energy into "making it happen" only to have it blow up in my face, and I would walk away from those moments feeling rejected and despondent like "God where are you in this?" "Did I act in emotions?"

You reading this may have experienced a similar situation. Maybe you experienced rejection through perceived failure or maybe like Hagar where you were subjected to someone in your home and instead of you receiving love and acceptance, you were despised. I encourage you today there will be people and circumstances in your life that will leave you feeling hurt and disappointed but look to Jesus, He is the door and entry way into your inner healing.

So just remember that the rejection you feel today can be the tool that God uses for your breakthrough tomorrow.

Do you see yourself in Sarah or do you see yourself in Hagar?

_____

_____

_____

_____

_____

_____

_____

How does knowing or hearing Hagar's story make you feel empowered?

_____

_____

_____

_____

_____

How are you seeing yourself in this story and what is your hope for the future?

_____

_____

_____

_____

_____

_____

MIRROR MOMENT:

So take a moment to think about a time in your life where rejection has shown up!

What idea and/or situation in your past experience would you say has contributed to your limited thinking and limited small belief in yourself? Knowing that God still has a plan for you does that make you feel empowered?

_____

_____

_____

_____

_____

_____

_____

_____

_____

_____

_____

_____

_____

_____

CHAPTER 5
I CHOOSE TO FORGIVE YOU!

MIRROR OF FORGIVENESS

Forgiveness: the action or process of forgiving or being forgiven.

This chapter was very hard for me to write. In all transparency I am literally still walking out my journey of forgiveness; it has been extremely hard for me because I am still learning how not to be so guarded in my personal relationships and making others pay for my past negative experiences of mistreatment and betrayal.

Forgiveness is extremely difficult but it is so necessary. The only one that can help you through this journey is Christ and YOU. You must be willing to get to the other side of the pain and betrayal.

I literally had to have a one on one with God to ask him to partner with me on this road to forgiveness because I didn't know how to do it on my own. A part of me wanted to let the betrayal go, but another part of me wanted to remain a victim…. Can you relate?

I know what it feels like to trust a devoted friend and have them violate my trust! I know what it feels like to give a family member too much access and to allow them to get too close only to feel that they used their proximity to you to stab you in the back. I know you reading this may be able to relate to my experience.

In the book of John, it shows how Jesus could relate first hand to what betrayal feels like with his relationship with Judas. It was up close and personal but controversial, you see, Jesus already knew that Judas would betray him because it was all a part of God's plan to bring world salvation through his son, but he also knew that without Judas he couldn't fulfill his calling. There was a friendship that was forged between the two of them so that Jesus could be revealed as the Messiah, but for him to also guide the 12 disciples into their own purpose to carry the gospel worldwide after his departure.

Here is when Jesus recognized his enemy …….

"I tell you the truth, one of you will betray me— one who is eating with me" (Mark 14:18). Notice that Jesus characterizes Judas' participation as a betrayal. And regarding accountability for this betrayal Jesus said, "Woe to that man who betrays the Son of Man! It would be better for him if he had not been born" (Mark 14:21)

We often quote this in our society today "What would Jesus do"; but we really don't take into consideration that He was all man and all God. I am pretty sure He felt exactly what we would feel in a similar situation; both hurt and disappointed, especially when you give someone access into your private life you would expect them to honor and respect the relationship.

I had a very similar situation happen to me where I allowed someone into my heart and my private space. At the time I felt that the person was trustworthy and integral; so I let my guard down, I opened up to this person with private conversation, thoughts and concerns only to find that this person was not interested in me but more so what I could offer them, so their access to me was with a hidden agenda and ulterior motive. I was later exploited and the information that was privately shared was rumored and used against me when I did not conform to their standards of our very close relationship. That experience caused me great pain and caused me to isolate myself. It left me unable to trust anyone and I would place a guard up with anyone who attempted to get close to me.

Much like Judas, there are some people who are close to you that don't have your best interest at heart. They are not for you; they are for themselves. Judas knew that Jesus was appointed by God as the savior of the world, yet he was more interested in what Jesus could provide for him in the form of association and connection more than him being invested in the relationship in itself. My Spiritual Sister Dr. Carrie Motley would often tell me, "Sis, we all need a Judas in our life; ultimately the betrayal that others commit against you will always work out for your good in the end." *Romans 8:28 (KJV) ... and we know that all things work together for the good to them that love God, to them who are CALLED according to HIS purpose.*

They may have meant to hurt you, but what the devil meant for evil, God will always turn it around to fit his perfect plan.

Forgiveness is a process and it doesn't happen overnight; but with much prayer, healing and trust in God it will get better. Jesus couldn't get to the cross without Judas and neither can you get to the other side of your hurt until you are willing to forgive those who have hurt you.

MIRROR MOMENT:

Take a few minutes and think about a situation or a circumstance in your own life where you forgave someone who hurt you deeply?

_____

_____

_____

_____

_____

_____

_____

_____

What were some of the steps you took in order to start the healing process?

_____

_____

_____

_____

_____

Did you receive an apology?

_____

_____

_____

_____

_____

If you received one have you been able to move on?

_____

_____

_____

_____

_____

CHAPTER 6
THIS HURTS SO BAD!

MIRROR OF GRIEF

I can't go on.

I can't believe they are gone.

I wish I had more time with them.

I should have done more.

Why them and why now?

How could this happen?

God why did this happen?

I was raised never to ask God why but; inevitably it is a question of the hearts of all mankind, 2020 was a year of isolation, uncertainty, panic and fear.

This past year alone we lost 2.72 million victims worldwide to the COVID19 virus. Over 22 million U.S. workers lost their jobs, racial tension, rioting and looting increased as a result of unresolved social injustice causing several small businesses and large corporations to close down permanently.

With all of these events happening simultaneously one after another, it didn't allow any of us to properly grieve the loss of our loved ones due to the strict CDC mandated quarantine measures throughout every city; many had to quickly bury their loved ones due to overcrowded hospitals and funeral homes. We don't have to wonder what that feels like because we all experienced the pandemic as a whole which brings me to the story of Job in the bible. Job was an upright and wealthy man, blameless before God but experienced extreme loss and grief all in the matter of one day not a year ....*1 day*!

Job had lost all of his sons, daughters, sheep, camels and servants and his body was stricken with infirmity and sickness. After hearing everything that had transpired, here was Job's response ....

> *Job 1:20-22*
>
> *At this, Job got up and tore his robe and shaved his head. Then he fell to the ground in worship and said:*

"Naked I came from my mother's womb,
and naked I will depart.
The Lord gave and the Lord has taken away;
may the name of the Lord be praised."
In all this, Job did not sin by charging God with
wrongdoing.

I myself have experienced sudden loss and grief in my family this past year in the loss of my brother "Charles Boyd King". His death has left a gaping hole in my heart which also had me in a space for months asking myself could I have done more. What were some crucial moments that I could have taken more seriously in order to maximize and spend more time with him? Grief will have you rehearsing these questions in your mind. His death was not attributed to the covid19 virus, but to a debilitating health condition that left him physically handicapped, making it extremely difficult to accomplish day to day tasks. This sickness consistently kept him in and out of the hospital for over 15 years, leaving him feeling weak and despondent; not having the physical energy to do much of anything. Some days were full of depression because he longed for a life of purpose and fulfillment. He would often say over our long phone conversations that he wanted to get married someday and have children. He was placed on this earth to be a creative/ artist. He was exceptionally talented in drawing and he would always encourage others to pursue their own talents and dreams to pursue those things that brought them joy.

He understood his limitations but still had the strength and ability to push someone else. He was a beacon of light in this dark world. He would constantly tell me he was proud of me and how he admired my drive and my pursuit of my calling.

Regret and grief causes is to reflect. They make you question the moments and conversations that you once shared with your loved ones. During the grief process you sometimes wonder things like, "Did I take the time that my brother and I had for granted? "I'm pretty sure Job had these same thoughts or even conversations behind closed doors but all of a sudden they held great meaning after the loss of his children. I'm sure it crossed his mind that there may have been some things that he could have done differently. Maybe he wished like me, that he could have spent more time with his children and perhaps created more memories.

Even though Job's loss was astronomically great, what stood out most to me in his story was how he maintained his conviction and commitment to God. Even after his wife had given up hope and told him to turn his back on God, even his friend turned their back on him and yet he remained faithful to God. If you reference the entire book, he had moments of doubt and even questions on why all this had happened to him, but he didn't allow his grief or heartache to overtake his relationship with God. Loss and grief are inevitable and will come knocking on your door someday. There is no running from it, but its effects can bring out the best or worst in us all. You may have lost a loved one and you can't seem to process it or you may have feelings of guilt, anger and even depression. Or maybe you lost your job /career and you poured yourself into that position day after day only to be given a note saying, "we have to let you go." Now, you are left trying to figure out how to pay your bills and support your family. Or maybe you have experienced loss in a relationship due to a heartbreaking divorce, your entire life is shattered and you are trying to find your way back to putting the pieces of your life back together again.

Grief will leave you numb, sad and even angry but your way through grief is to give yourself permission to feel these emotions and express them with someone you trust like a certified family therapist, a trusted friend and even in open dialogue through conversation with God.

What grief has taught me in the loss of my brother is doing life with a strict calendar full of to- do's, work demands, operating a full-time business, operating in my ministry calling, working on my marriage , and raising my kids . Will sometimes have to be put aside in order to make time for special moments and opportunities to build lasting relationships with those you love because tomorrow is truly not promised.

Grief has also taught me to be patient and allow time for healing through the process and if you invite God and others in to help carry the load, you won't be left to travel the journey of grief alone.

The human experience is so complex and if we can learn how to navigate all these different highs and lows; mountains and valleys without losing sight of who God says we are, if we can go through life and maintain the belief and transformation of his word, we can be more than conquerors, but there are times when we tend to forget because the pain is so heavy and the last thing you wanna hear when you're going through it is what "God said." It can seem a little insensitive but his word still remains true "*He is nigh until those with a broken heart and saves the contrite and wounded*" though you may feel alone in your grief you are not alone sis, this is collective, we're in this together and more than that God is with us.

Take a moment to become more aware of the different Stages of Grief:

1. Denial

2. Bargaining

3. Acceptance

4. Sadness/Depression: allow these feelings to move through you understanding that it is all a part of the healing process

5. Anger

Where are you in your grief process?

_____

_____

_____

_____

_____

_____

_____

_____

Local Support & Resources Available To You:

- Look into your local community outreach center or church, they may have 1 on 1 Christian counseling

- Connect with someone that has a similar story but has made it on the other side of it, to assist you during this difficult time

- Private Mirror Work FB Group

  www.griefresourcenetwork.com

  www.cdc.gov

MIRROR MOMENT:

Where do you see yourself in Job's story?

_____

_____

_____

_____

_____

_____

_____

_____

How did going through COVID 19 pandemic negatively or positively affected you?

_____

_____

_____

_____

_____

_____

_____

How can you use your grief or situation in order to help someone else that may have experienced major loss in their life?

_____

_____

_____

_____

_____

_____

_____

_____

_____

CHAPTER 7
ATTACHMENTS VS ASSIGNMENTS

MIRROR OF RELATIONSHIPS

Attachment: a deep and enduring emotional bond between two people in which each seeks closeness and feels more secure when in the presence of the attachment figure.

Assignment: the attribution of someone or something as The story of Joseph and his brother are the perfect example of attachments versus assignments.

He was attached to his brothers by blood but he was assigned by God to bring his entire family out of poverty. At the age of 17 he was called to be a visionary and leader, but his brothers resented him for the dream given to him by God. He was shown in a visual that he would do great things in his life but he made one mistake, he thought he could entrust his dreams with his own flesh and blood and all along they couldn't be trusted and even conspired together to kill him once they knew that he had Purpose on his life; does this sound familiar? There are people in our lives who we feel can be trusted solely based on the fact that they are family, but this is a sure sign that trust has to be earned even within families. Ultimately, the plan of GOD was unfolding, instead of them killing him they sold him in to slavery in Egypt.

Here is how the masterful plan of God unfolded **Genesis 45:4-11NIV…...**

> *Then Joseph said to his brothers, "Come close to me." When they had done so, he said, "I am your brother Joseph, the one you sold into Egypt!*
>
> *And now, do not be distressed and do not be angry with yourselves for selling me here, because it was to save lives that God sent me ahead of you.*
>
> *For two years now there has been famine in the land, and for the next five years there will be no plowing and reaping.*

But God sent me ahead of you to preserve for you a remnant on earth and to save your lives by a great deliverance.

So then, it was not you who sent me here, but God. He made me father to Pharaoh, lord of his entire household and ruler of all Egypt. Now hurry back to my father and say to him, 'this is what your son Joseph says: God has made me lord of all Egypt. Come down to me; don't delay. You shall live in the region of Goshen and be near me—you, your children and grandchildren, your flocks and herds, and all you have. I will provide for you there, because five years of famine are still to come. Otherwise, you and your household and all who belong to you will become destitute.

Imagine how they must have felt realizing that their plan to kill their brother had ultimately failed but what they meant for evil God turned it around for the good of not only Joseph but them and their entire family.

No good ever comes out of hatred and jealousy. It causes us to live in fear, make assumptions, and dread whatever is or isn't to come. We can all learn a lesson from Joseph's brothers. Instead of letting jealousy rule us, we can ask for God's peace to take over that space in our hearts. When we trust Him with our lives, we don't have to fall into the pit of jealousy and strife. We all have our own unique purpose and remember it will never be identical to anyone else's.

God called them out of poverty and prepared a place for them and Joseph could have been bitter, angry and unforgiving but he understood that God had called him to wealth through his connection and relationship with pharaoh which was the very thing God used in order to pull his family out of poverty.

Have you considered that God can be repositioning you by allowing certain trials in your life to transpire? The same people that are conspiring against you are the same ones you are called to break generational curses for, how we manage people is so critical to our destiny, you never know who is tied to your destiny, the enemy uses fear but God uses PEOPLE.

MIRROR MOMENT:

Take a moment to examine your five closest relationships. Are they attachments or assignments?

_____

_____

_____

_____

_____

_____

_____

Does your current relationships drain you or inspire you?

_____

_____

_____

_____

_____

_____

Are you growing or do you feel stagnant?

_____

_____

_____

_____

_____

_____

_____

How do you manage people in your life?

_____

_____

_____

_____

_____

_____

_____

CHAPTER 8
WHY ME?

MIRROR OF TRAUMA

Me: They won't believe me!

I want my daddy!

I can't let them in because they will hurt me!

I don't trust them!

Do they really love me?

I will be okay by myself. I don't need them!

I have to protect myself because no one else did.

Them: I was hurt as a child too.

No one ever told me they loved me.

My dad was never there for me.

I had to figure out life on my own.

I was left alone with a family member I thought was trustworthy but they violated me too.

51

Does this sound familiar?

To the little girl who was molested or neglected, you consistently show up in your marriage and even very close relationships guarded because you never really healed from your childhood neglect or your childhood trauma, now you are self-sabotaging those who try to get close to you through because you don't know how to open up and trust others.

A lot of times trauma stems from unresolved childhood neglect or abuse.

I was that young girl violated at an early age and I asked God why and what I did to deserve that type of hurt. The void and pain of this traumatic experience left me shattered. I constantly cried for my now deceased father Michael King who at that time did not have the mental or physical capacity to save me from this pain because he was dealing with his own inner demons of depression and alcoholism. Who could help me if my own father couldn't? So that left me with daddy issues of abandonment. I was lost and wounded after being molested as a child. The brokenness I felt transcended across all of my relationships. Going into my dating life as a young adult, I was filled with insecurities and a constant need for affirmation. If I felt like I wasn't genuinely loved and protected or receiving the constant attention I needed, I would move on quickly. I did not allow anyone to enter that place where they could further wound my heart, which left no room for healing, growth or resolutions. My friendships were few and far in between because females to me were difficult to deal with and super flaky and superficial.

At the time I didn't recognize that I judged women harshly because the same way that I looked at them was what I was internalizing within myself, I realized that the thing I was most afraid of was the very energy I was putting out. I spent my entire young adult life hiding behind, " I'm good or I will be okay," "I'm not about to beg anyone to love me", when in fact I wasn't okay. I was wounded and I needed to allow the wound that was still open from childhood to finally heal.

It wasn't until I was 37 years old that I finally decided to take my life in a different direction and that took a lot of guts and self-examination; I had suppressed all of my pain for a season and had dedicated all of myself into becoming a very successful business woman after all that was all I knew. I had come from a household where entrepreneurship and education were the status quo and measuring stick. I was born and raised in church, so I knew how to cry out to God for help, but this situation left me feeling ashamed and abandoned by God because I suffered for so long in this cycle of trauma.

My childhood pain would show up in my life during times that I felt hurt, unprotected and insecure. I believe Apostle Paul could understand firsthand what trauma felt like In the book of 2 Corinthians 11:23-29. He had to endure great hardship during his journey to preach the gospel around the world.

> *"I have worked much harder, been in prison more frequently, been flogged more severely, and been exposed to death again and again. Five times I received from the Jews the forty lashes minus one. Three times I was beaten with rods, once I was pelted with stones, three times I was shipwrecked, I spent a night and a day in the open sea, I have been constantly on the move. I have been in danger from rivers, in danger in the country, in*

danger at sea; and in danger from false believers. I have labored and toiled and have often gone without sleep; I have known hunger and thirst and have often gone without food; I have been cold and naked. Besides everything else, I face daily the pressure of my concern for all the churches."

Trauma comes in all shapes and forms, it doesn't stop by to announce itself but slowly it gets buried deep inside your heart and at the moment you least expect it, it starts to show up in your behaviors and even in how you make your day-to-day decisions.

Peter A. Levine, Ph.D., who has treated and researched trauma for over 45 years, says,

> *The effects of unresolved trauma can be devastating. It can affect our habits and outlook on life, leading to addictions and poor decision-making. It can take a toll on our family life and interpersonal relationships. It can trigger real physical pain, symptoms, and disease. And it can lead to a range of self-destructive behaviors.*

I am now on the other side of the traumatic experiences that I endured and I know that I am a better woman because of it, but the little 10 year old girl in me sometimes still wonders what if I never experienced the molestation, trauma and pain, would I have lived a different life? , Would I still be the same person I am today? Would I have taken a different path for my life?

And my answer back is, "girl you had to go through that experience, it made you more compassionate towards others who have experienced the same hurt in their own lives, it also made you stronger, wiser, and able to discern those relationships closest to you, to recognize if the motives are pure as well as those I have chosen to invite into my life,"

My past has helped me to realize my power through the pain and helped me to be more self-aware and more protective and discerning of who has access to my heart.

Here are 10 ways to know if you have unresolved trauma in your life.

- Anxiety or panic attacks
- A feeling of shame; an innate feeling that you are bad, worthless, or without importance
- Suffering from chronic or ongoing depression

- Practicing avoidance of people, places, or things that may be related to the traumatic event; including an avoidance of unpleasant emotions

- Flashbacks and nightmares regarding the traumatic event

- Addiction and eating disorder in an attempt to escape or numb negative emotions

- Sleeping issues including trouble going to sleep or staying asleep

- Suffering from feelings of detachment, or feeling "numb inside"

- Suicidal thought or actions

- Uncontrollable anger; acting on it

- Not being able to tolerate conflicts

If you identify with any, or all of these then you may want to ask yourself if it's time to talk with a spiritual mentor, counselor, or even a Christian therapist about your trauma. Is it easier to function as you are, or to work through the pain you have suffered? It's a question that only you can answer, but rest assured, you are not alone.

There are many people who have been traumatized, may even have developed PTSD who have worked through the events of their past, and recovered. There is help and support out there for them and for YOU.

MIRROR MOMENT:

So how are the broken pieces of you showing up in your adult life?

_____

_____

_____

_____

_____

What are some of the things you never healed from as a child that are now showing up in your marriage, relationships , business, or even the way you parent your children?

_____

_____

_____

_____

What has trauma taught you?

_____

_____

_____

_____

_____

_____

_____

How can you use the trauma you have experienced in your life to help someone else overcome their traumatic past?

_____

_____

_____

_____

_____

_____

_____

CHAPTER 9
MIRROR OF PAIN

Everyone hates to suffer, but the fact of the matter is that PAIN CHANGES US. It's not meant to make us weak; it's designed to make us stronger. When we go through pain in life it heals us.

2 Corinthians 4:16-18; that's why we are not discouraged. No, even if outwardly we are wearing out, inwardly we are being renewed each and every day. This light, temporary nature of our suffering is producing for us an everlasting weight of glory, far beyond any comparison, because we do not look for things that can be seen but for things that cannot be seen. For things that can be seen are temporary, but things that cannot be seen are eternal.

Think of pain while exercising. It might hurt, but you are becoming stronger in the process. More weights equals more pain. More pain equals more strength.

Even a pregnant woman can attest to feeling excruciating physical pains and emotional distress during the birthing process as her body is adjusting to bringing forth a new baby into the world. The baby is born she forgets the pain and embraces her new bundle of joy.

Pain is inevitable and a part of life.

When I think of how olive oil is made the purpose of the crushing and bruising of the olive is to facilitate the release of the oil from the vacuoles. All the while God is allowing the pain in your life in order to purify, sanctify and anoint the vessel to be used by Him.

It might be hard, but we must find joy in and through our pain.

You may ask, "How do I do that?" We must seek Christ.

These are the questions we have to ask ourselves.

How can this painful situation help to make me more like Christ?

_____

_____

_____

_____

_____

_____

_____

_____

How can this be used to help others?

_____

_____

_____

_____

_____

_____

_____

_____

_____

Whether you are in pain due to a situation out of your control, physical illness or emotional distress, seek your help through God **JEHOVAH NISSI**

My Banner.......who is our Almighty Healer. You will find everlasting comfort, peace and encouragement in His word. He knows what you're going through and He will not leave you in this alone.

The storm you are in right now didn't come to stay but this too shall pass.

The masterful plan of God will be revealed in time but until then hold on and don't give up there is "PURPOSE IN YOUR PAIN".

MIRROR MOMENTS:

What has been your coping mechanism when dealing with pain?

_____

_____

_____

_____

_____

Do you see the purpose in your pain?

_____

_____

_____

_____

_____

_____

_____

_____

What is the root cause of your pain?

_____

_____

_____

_____

_____

_____

_____

_____

As we navigate through life there are many things that we encounter that help to shape us, teach us, mold us and prepare us for greater purpose. Some situations leave us wounded internally while others may leave physical scars to remind us of what we've survived. What I know for sure is that while some of the painful and life altering situations that we have faced may not have been our faults, healing is 100 percent our responsibility. No matter where you find yourself in your life today, you owe it to yourself to heal from your past, release the things that you cannot control so that you can live a purposeful and abundant life. You are worth the tender love, care, commitment and concern required to face and tend to your inner turmoil. You deserve peace and functionality. Decide today to commit to the best version of yourself by first taking a long look in the mirror and choosing to work on yourself. You are the most important project that you will ever get to work on.

Devote the next 21 days to devotion, reflection, prayer and healing.

Start your 21-day Mirror Work Journey with these powerful "I AM" statements. Declare these words over your life each day as you work on evolving into the best version of yourself.

Mirror Talk 21 "I Am Statements":

Before we start our 21-day journey I want you to begin with "Mirror Talk "I want you to stand in the mirror and repeat these words to yourself.

I am saved

I am righteous

I am a child of God

I am whole

I am victorious

I am healed

I am strong

I am wise

I am walking in my purpose

I am a miracle

I am fearless

I am blessed

I am confident

I am made in his image

I am worthy

I am grounded in loved

I am protected

I am faithful

I am resilient

I am beautiful

I am a trailblazer

21 DAYS OF
AFFIRMATION

DAY ONE

Affirmation: I declare and decree that I will remain focused and in a state of gratitude for the "NOW" I will meditate on how the love and grace of God is sufficient for today. I denounce all feelings of fear, anxiety and uncertainties which come in the form of outside noise, distractions and future to-do's trying to pull me away from what is really important in this present moment and that is PEACE!

In Jesus Name.

Confession Scripture.

> *Isaiah 26:3 KJV*
>
> *"Thou wilt keep him in perfect peace, whose mind is stayed on thee: because he trusteth in thee."*

MIRROR WORK:

What will you do differently today in order to change your current circumstances and/or situation?

_____

_____

_____

_____

_____

_____

_____

_____

_____

_____

_____

_____

DAY TWO

I declare and decree that I won't allow my past failures, hurts or disappointments to keep me from experiencing the miracle that God wants to perform in my life today. Through his divine love for me and through the multiple expressions of his tender mercies toward me.

In Jesus Name.

Confession Scripture:

> *Romans 8:38-39 (KJV)*
> *"For I am persuaded, that neither death, nor life, nor angels, nor principalities, nor powers, nor things present, nor things to come,"*
> *"Nor height, nor depth, nor any other creature, shall be able to separate us from the love of God, which is in Christ Jesus our Lord."*

MIRROR WORK:

What will you do differently today in order to deal with your past hurt, failures and disappointments?

_____

_____

_____

_____

_____

_____

_____

_____

_____

_____

_____

_____

_____

_____

_____

DAY THREE

I declare and decree that I won't allow worry and discontentment to rob me of my joy today. I choose to praise God through this present moment of uncertainty and I am settled in the fact that He has my life in the palm of his hands, He has all the answers to the questions that deeply concern me.

In Jesus Name.

Confession Scripture:

> *Philippians 4:6-7 (NKJV)*
>
> *Be anxious for nothing, but in everything by prayer and supplication, with thanksgiving, let your requests be made known to God; and the peace of God, which surpasses all understanding, will guard your hearts and minds through Christ Jesus.*

MIRROR WORK:

What will you do differently today in order to not allow worry or lack to consume you?

_____

_____

_____

_____

_____

_____

_____

_____

_____

_____

_____

_____

_____

_____

_____

_____

DAY FOUR

I declare and decree that I will speak what God has said about me and not mentally rehearse or verbally repeat what someone else has negativity said concerning me. I take authority and dominion over my actions and my thoughts. I command the fruit of my lips to produce what I want to see good happening in my life. I have the VICTORY!

In Jesus Name.

Confession Scripture:

> *Proverbs 18:21 (KJV)*
> *Death and life are in the power of the tongue: and they that love it shall eat the fruit thereof.*

MIRROR WORK:

What will you do differently today in order to have the things that you say?

_____

_____

_____

_____

_____

_____

_____

_____

_____

_____

_____

_____

_____

_____

_____

DAY FIVE

I declare that my times are in his hands. I decree that I will not get ahead of the Lord, but will remain rooted in the fact that I have been chosen, anointed and appointed by God to carry out the work that He has assigned for me to accomplish in the earth. I denounce any feelings of inferiority or self-sabotage, and in turn I praise God for He already knows the end before the beginning. I am an Overcomer!

In Jesus Name.

Confession Scripture:

> *Jeremiah 26:4 (KJV)*
> *As for me, behold, I am in your hand: do with me as seemeth good and meet unto you.*

MIRROR WORK:

What will you do today in order to stay in the perfect will of God for your life?

_____

_____

_____

_____

_____

_____

_____

_____

_____

_____

_____

_____

_____

_____

_____

DAY SIX

I declare and decree that today the "FAVOR" of God is looking for me. There is a table being prepared right in the presence of my enemies, My God desires to bless me. I am the apple of His eye; I am His delight. He is seeking and looking for ways to be good to me.

The promises of the Lord are sure, and His mercies from everlasting to everlasting.

In Jesus Name

Confession Scripture:

> *1 Corinthians 2:9 (KJV)*
> *But as it is written, Eye hath not seen, nor ear heard, neither have entered into the heart of man, the things which God hath prepared for them that love him.*

MIRROR WORK:

What will you do today in order to keep your eyes solely on God and not on the problem?

_____

_____

_____

_____

_____

_____

_____

_____

_____

_____

_____

_____

_____

_____

_____

_____

DAY SEVEN

I declare and decree new miracles, and break through blessings over all of my relationships, my family, loved ones and friends. God is not only doing a "NEW" thing in my life but also in those who are connected to me.

I thank you in advance Father for what you are about to do in this season in the lives of those I love; and we know that your desire for your children is for us to serve you with our whole heart and through our servitude you will bless us with your unfailing love and tender mercies.

In Jesus Name!

Confession Scripture:

> *Isaiah 43:19*
> *Behold, I will do a new thing; now it shall spring forth; shall ye not know it? I will even make a way in the wilderness, and rivers in the desert.*

MIRROR WORK:

What are willing to sacrifice and put down in order to receive the new thing God has for you?

_____

_____

_____

_____

_____

_____

_____

_____

_____

_____

_____

_____

_____

_____

_____

_____

_____

DAY EIGHT

I declare and decree that today I will allow laughter to consume every part of me in every place in my life that wants to bring me low in depression and despair, I choose to put on the garment of praise and to see the glass half full instead of half empty, it is surely the Lord that is the lifter of my head ... so I laugh at the enemy because God has the final say in this chapter of my life, and this I know for sure that it is not over until God says it is over.

In Jesus Name, Amen

Confession Scripture:

> *Psalm 37:13*
> *The Lord shall laugh at him: for He seeth that his day is coming*

MIRROR WORK:

What will you do today in order to invite joy and happiness back into your life?

_____

_____

_____

_____

_____

_____

_____

_____

_____

_____

_____

_____

_____

_____

_____

_____

DAY NINE

I declare and decree that I am taking back everything that has been stolen from me; even some of things I gave away due to being negligent, self-sabotage, and ignorant to the devices of satan. God is restoring me and giving it all back. The plans of the enemy have failed and the fiery darts that were sent to take me out did not and will not prosper.

In Jesus Name, Amen

Confession Scripture:

> *Joel 2:25*
> *So, I will restore to you the years that the swarming locust has eaten,*
> *The crawling locust,*
> *The consuming locust,*
> *And the chewing locust,*
> *My great army which I sent among you.*

MIRROR WORK:

What will you do today in order to regain your losses and secure your wins?

_____

_____

_____

_____

_____

_____

_____

_____

_____

_____

_____

_____

_____

_____

_____

DAY TEN

I declare and decree my entire household is secure, whole, saved and filled with the Holy Ghost.

As for me and my house we will serve the Lord, and there is no weapon that is formed against us that will prosper. What was intended to harm us will fall to the ground, vengeance belongs to God, and He will repay all.

I have the victory! In Jesus Name, Amen

Confession Scripture:

> *Exodus 4:14*
> *The LORD shall fight for you, and ye shall hold your peace*

MIRROR WORK:

What will you do today in order to stand in faith and victory for your family?

_____

_____

_____

_____

_____

_____

_____

_____

_____

_____

_____

_____

_____

_____

_____

DAY ELEVEN

I decree and declare that God will provide all that I lack and stand in need of this day!

He has promised me that I am the head and not the tail, that I am the lender and not the borrower, so I stand in agreement with God and His word that he is working it all out for my good but for his excellent glory. My situation is already looking better.

In Jesus Name, Amen

Confession Scripture:

> *Philippians 4:19*
> *But my God shall supply all your need according to his riches in glory by Christ Jesus*

MIRROR WORK:

What can you do today in order to take control of your finances, walk in abundance and plan to prosper?

_____

_____

_____

_____

_____

_____

_____

_____

_____

_____

_____

_____

_____

_____

_____

_____

DAY TWELVE

I declare and decree that I will stay faithful today!

When it gets extremely difficult, and life happens, while I don't always see the handiwork of God; I have decided to stand on His promises and trust in this process. I know I am still a work in progress and He will finish the work that He started in me.

In Jesus Name, Amen

Confession Scripture:

> *Philippians 1:6 (NKJV)*
> *Being confident of this very thing, that He who has begun a good work in you will complete it until the day of Jesus Christ*

MIRROR WORK:

What will you do today in order to trust God; while you wait?

_____

_____

_____

_____

_____

_____

_____

_____

_____

_____

_____

_____

_____

_____

_____

_____

DAY THIRTEEN

I declare and decree mercy, truth and goodness are my portion today. Everything that was sent to upset or destroy me will fail. I call on the angelic host of the Lord to invade my atmosphere. I bind and rebuke the satanic attack sent against me and I plead the blood of Jesus.

In Jesus Name, Amen

Confession Scripture:

> *James 4:7*
>
> *Submit yourselves therefore to God. Resist the devil, and he will flee from you.*

MIRROR WORK:

What can you do today in order to remain in peace?

_____

_____

_____

_____

_____

_____

_____

_____

_____

_____

_____

_____

_____

_____

_____

_____

_____

_____

DAY FOURTEEN

I declare and decree that today will be the day that I see the mighty hand of God work in my life. The word states that God is pleased by our faith in Him, so I choose to be patient and not waver nor doubt, because what I see in the natural is only temporary. He is faithful to his promises and He will not fail me.

In Jesus name, Amen

Confession Scripture:

> *Philippians 4:6-7*
> *New King James Version*
> *Be anxious for nothing, but in everything by prayer and supplication, with thanksgiving, let your requests be made known to God; and the peace of God, which surpasses all understanding, will guard your hearts and minds through Christ Jesus.*

MIRROR WORK:

What in your life triggers anxiety and worry?

_____

_____

_____

_____

_____

_____

_____

_____

_____

_____

_____

_____

_____

_____

_____

_____

DAY FIFTEEN

I declare and decree the plans of God will stand in my life. Though things may not always go according to my plans, I will rest in the fact that God has it all in His hands. I invite the Holy Spirit to lead and guide me today. I am free to walk in the newness of life. Lord, fall afresh on me I am open to receive.

In Jesus Name, Amen

Confession Scripture:

> *Proverbs 16:9*
> *King James Version*
> *A man's heart deviseth his way: but the Lord directeth his steps.*

MIRROR WORK:

What or who in your life is holding you back from fulfilling your greatest potential?

_____

_____

_____

_____

_____

_____

_____

_____

_____

_____

_____

_____

_____

_____

_____

DAY SIXTEEN

I declare and decree that I am ready! When my prayer is answered, and the opportunity presents itself I will not be getting ready because "I Am Ready" I will not be lazy, comfortable or complacent, but working by faith with works expecting the unexpected.

In Jesus Name, Amen

Confession Scripture:

> *Proverbs 13:4*
> *The soul of the sluggard craves and gets nothing,*
> *while the soul of the diligent is richly supplied.*

MIRROR WORK:

What areas in your life can you see opportunities for growth?

_____

_____

_____

_____

_____

_____

_____

_____

_____

_____

_____

_____

_____

_____

_____

_____

DAY SEVENTEEN

I declare and decree that today I walk in total healing. All power and dominion have been given to me to speak out of my mouth what I want to see happen in my life. And so, I speak that my body is healed, my mind is free and my spirit is complete and whole.

In Jesus Name, Amen

Confession Scripture:

> *Isaiah 53:5*
>
> *But he was wounded for our transgressions, he was bruised for our iniquities: the chastisement of our peace was upon him; and with his stripes we are healed.*

MIRROR WORK:

What scars are you hiding that God wants to expose to start the healing process in your life?

_____

_____

_____

_____

_____

_____

_____

_____

_____

_____

_____

_____

_____

_____

_____

_____

DAY EIGHTEEN

I declare and decree that I will not allow frustration or confusion to rule my day but I take control, authority and dominion over my thought life and I speak the peace of God over me. Lord, you are the lifter of my head and the captain of my soul.

In Jesus Name!

Confession Scripture:

> *1 Corinthians 2:16*
> *For who hath known the mind of the Lord, that he may instruct him? But we have the mind of Christ.*

MIRROR WORK:

Set your intentions on the good things that are possible for your life. What good things do you choose to focus on today?

_____

_____

_____

_____

_____

_____

_____

_____

_____

_____

_____

_____

_____

_____

_____

_____

DAY NINETEEN

I declare and decree that my family is protected and walking in freedom; every bloodline connection to me will find their God given purpose in and through Christ and be filled with the Holy Spirit; Satan will never be able to lay claim to my family as we all have been called to holiness and righteousness

In Jesus Name!

Confession Scripture:

> *Psalm 103:17-18*
> *New International Version*
> *But from everlasting to everlasting*
> *The Lord's love is with those who fear him, and his righteousness with their children's children with those who keep his covenant and remember to obey his precepts.*

MIRROR WORK:

How can you begin to build a family legacy? How can you bring your family together to begin to build something substantial for future generations?

_____

_____

_____

_____

_____

_____

_____

_____

_____

_____

_____

_____

_____

_____

_____

_____

DAY TWENTY

I declare and decree that all of my needs are met. The Lord has promised that He will give me the desires of my heart if I walk up right before Him, I am not perfect but I know that through Christ I am a new creature and as I continue to walk in Faith, God will perfect the things concerning me.

In Jesus Name!

Confession Scripture:

> *Jeremiah 46:7*
> *"But as for you, O Jacob My servant, do not fear,*
> *Nor be dismayed, O Israel!*
> *For, see, I am going to save you from afar,*
> *And your descendants from the land of their captivity;*
> *And Jacob will return and be undisturbed And secure, with no one making him tremble*

MIRROR WORK:

What are the current needs that you have placed before God? Is it financial? Spiritual? Or Physical? How would you like to see the spirit of Christ show up in your time of need?

_____

_____

_____

_____

_____

_____

_____

_____

_____

_____

_____

_____

_____

_____

DAY TWENTY-ONE

I declare and decree that my harvest time has come. I have been committed to the plans of God, I trust the Lord to enlarge my territory and strengthen my borders because of my obedience to God in this season. I receive every blessing that has my name attached to it.

In Jesus Name!

Confession Scripture:

> *Matthew 25:23*
> *His lord said unto him, Well done, good and faithful servant; thou hast been faithful over a few things, I will make thee ruler over many things: enter thou into the joy of thy lord.*

MIRROR WORK:

A season of well-kept seeds will produce a time of harvest. Many don't realize that the harvest is where the real work must commence. What seeds are you planting in faith? What will be the work required to manifest a plentiful harvest?

_____

_____

_____

_____

_____

_____

_____

_____

_____

_____

_____

_____

_____

_____

ABOUT THE AUTHOR

Christina King Rogers is a woman after God's Own heart. She stands for holiness and righteousness from humble beginnings, Christina has overcome emotional and sexual abuse, a major health crisis, mental break down, trauma, and low self-worth and where most would have fallen and given up through the grace of God she has risen above every challenge and obstacle in her life.

After being delivered from these various things, she felt it necessary to create a platform where women wouldn't have to suffer alone but be empowered and encouraged through every obstacle placed before them "Be Made Whole with Christina Ministries Inc" was birthed in her heart in 2017 as a vehicle for transformation, healing, and wholeness to take place in the soul of every woman.

As a "Young Emerging Prophetic Voice" for our nation she is compelled to reach the lost, teach and evangelize as the Lord leads the scope of her message extends beyond the pulpit and the heartbeat of her ministry flows to broken and hurting people.

Her path and journey hasn't been easy, but through the help and power of the Holy Ghost she is here as a testimony that Jesus Christ does indeed save, deliver and set free.

Owner of Blessed Organic Essentials LLC. An all-natural plant based skin care line and Whole International Inc., Non-Profit Community Based Organization. She has achieved Chicago High Honoree Recognition, Panelist for the Chicago Black Woman's Expo" Beauty, Branding

& Blogging Segment" Product Feature at the 2017 Grammy Awards, Contributing Writer in Mind Blowing Magazine, product featured in British Vogue Magazine.

Christina currently holds her Bachelor's Degree in Psychology from National Louis University Chicago, Illinois. She is the honored and Beloved Wife of Mercedes Rogers, Mother of 4, Author, Entrepreneur, Business Owner, Evangelist, Thought Leader, Mentor and most importantly an ambassador and servant of Jesus Christ.

She is humbly submitted under the Leadership of Superintendent David A. Reed; Reed's Temple COGIC Griffith, Indiana.

To Connect with Christina,
follow her on all media handles
@bemadewholeckr

FB @ChristinaKingRogers and visit
www.wholeinternationalinc.org

Made in the USA
Middletown, DE
09 June 2021